SNEAKER CENTURY

A HISTORY OF ATHLETIC SHOES

AMBER J. KEYSER

TWENTY-FIRST CENTURY BOOKS / MINNEAPOLIS

This book is dedicated to my dad, John Keyser, who always shares his love of sports, and to my grandfather, Joe Keyser, who watched Jesse Owens run at the 1936 Olympics in Berlin. I want to thank D'Wayne Edwards and Eric Graham, for sharing their sneaker expertise, and my writing group, Viva Scriva, for helping me find the story.

A note to readers about capitalization in this book: For the educational market, the publisher has chosen to capitalize Adidas when referring to the company and its shoes. The official name of the company is adidas. Additionally, athletic shoes manufactured by the company NIKE, Inc., are officially designated as Nike shoes. This book makes that stylistic distinction.

Twenty-First Century Books
A division of Lerner Publishing Group, Inc.
241 First Avenue North
Minneapolis, MN 55401 USA

For reading levels and more information, look up this title at www.lernerbooks.com.

Main body text set in Adrianna Regular 11/15.
Typeface provided by Chank Fonts.

Library of Congress Cataloging-in-Publication Data

Keyser, Amber.
      Sneaker century : a history of athletic shoes / by Amber J. Keyser.
         pages   cm.
      Includes bibliographical references and index.
      ISBN 978-1-4677-2640-5 (lib. bdg. : alk. paper)
      ISBN 978-1-4677-6309-7 (eBook)
      1. Sneakers. 2. Sneakers—Social aspects. I. Title.
   GV749.S64K49 2015
   685'.31—dc23   2014003214

Manufactured in the United States of America
1 – DP – 12/31/14

TABLE OF CONTENTS

prologue
FLU SHOES

Preston Truman's mom had tried to clean the red-and-black basketball shoes, but he rescued them. Those scuffed size thirteens with the autograph scrawled across one toe were something special—a piece of history. They didn't smell like sweat or the waxy polish of a basketball court. These sneakers smelled of victory. And Truman wasn't the only one who thought so.

In 2013 Truman pulled the shoes out of the safe-deposit box at a local bank where he had stored them for sixteen years. He contacted Grey Flannel Auctions, an auction house that specializes in sports memorabilia, and the bidding began. In the end, an anonymous collector bought them for $104,765.

That's a lot of money for a pair of sneakers, but those Nike Air Jordans weren't just any shoes. They were superstar basketball player Michael Jordan's famous flu shoes.

When Truman first met Jordan, it was 1996, and Truman was a teenage ball boy at the Delta Center Arena in Salt Lake City, Utah. Jordan, the star player for the Chicago Bulls, was suiting up for a regular season basketball game against the Utah Jazz, and he wasn't happy. The man wanted graham crackers and applesauce, but the sauce had gone AWOL. Jordan turned to Truman and teased, "There will be no autographs for ball boys after the game if I don't get my applesauce."

Truman was off like a shot, casing the sports facility for the goods, finally hitting pay dirt in a food storage room. Jordan got his snack, and Truman had made a friend.

Seven months later, the Bulls were back in Utah for the 1997 National Basketball Association (NBA) Finals.

Michael Jordan (*left*) didn't let a bout of the flu stop him from playing in a crucial game in the 1997 NBA Finals—with his beloved red-and-black Nike sneakers.

Again, Truman was working in the visiting team's locker room. This time, he had graham crackers and applesauce ready and waiting for Jordan, who remembered the teenager from before.

After the fourth game in the series, the Jazz had won two games and the Bulls had won two games. Game 5 would be pivotal. The winner would need just one more victory to clinch the best-of-seven series. However, Jordan had the flu and was so sick he could barely walk, much less play ball. His medical team told him to stay in bed, but instead, Jordan dragged himself to the locker room. Three hours before game time, Jordan was in a darkened back room, eyes closed, hooked up to an IV for fluids, visualizing what he had to do to win the game.

Finally, Jordan decided he could play—barely.

He slumped on the bench. He stumbled on and off the court. He could hardly run, and he nearly passed out. At times his teammates literally held him up. Team doctors told him he needed to stay out of the game, but the Jazz were ahead and Jordan didn't like to lose.

From some unknown reserve of strength, Jordan went deep, played harder, ran faster. In the final thirty seconds of the game, the score was tied. Teammate Scottie Pippen passed to Jordan, who nailed a three-pointer and collapsed into Pippen's arms. That shot sent the series back to Chicago, where the Bulls would win the sixth game and secure their fifth NBA title.

Truman, who had brought applesauce at halftime and wrapped a towel around Jordan's shoulders at the end, knew he was seeing history. After the game, Jordan unlaced his sneakers, signed them, and gave them to Truman, who kept them under lock and key until the 2013 auction.

The story of the flu shoes encapsulates all aspects of sneakers today: heroic athletes and dedicated fans, style and technology, big business and even bigger money. In just over a century, since they were first invented in the late 1800s, sneakers and sneaker culture have swept across the globe, capturing our hearts—and our feet.

chapter 1
THE FIRST SNEAKERS

Sneakers are everywhere. Whether they are full of holes, covered in bling, or in mint condition, sneakers are the go-to shoe for people around the world, especially kids and teens. Check out the halls at school or the food court at the mall, and you'll see sneakers on most of the feet in those places. They come in hundreds of colors, low-tops and high-tops, laced-up, laceless, and unlaced. You can even get high-heeled sneakers. The dedicated, sometimes obsessed fans of athletic shoes proudly call themselves sneaker freaks or sneakerheads.

So what's with this footwear craze? For that matter, what makes a sneaker a sneaker?

Whether you call them kicks or trainers, tennies or athletic shoes, you're still talking about a shoe that's pretty basic—just a rubber sole and a lightweight upper. Sneakers have gone more high tech over the years, but the truth is, these humble shoes aren't that much different now than they were when they were first invented.

The real question is, how did sneakers take over the world?

Sagebrush Sandals and Sheep Dung Moccasins

For tens of thousands of years, our early human ancestors made two kinds of shoes. Platform-style shoes consisted of a sole held onto the foot with straps, much like a sandal. Wrap-style shoes, or moccasins, were made of leather or fabric that wrapped around the foot.

In 1938 anthropologist and archaeologist Luther Cressman was working in the high desert region of Central Oregon. He was digging his way through layers of dust, pack rat droppings, and ash from an ancient volcanic eruption when he uncovered the oldest platform-style shoe ever found—a ten-thousand-year-old sandal made of twisted sagebrush bark.

Decades later, in 2008, graduate student Diana Zardaryan found the oldest wrap-style shoe while excavating a cave in Armenia called Areni-1. The fifty-five-hundred-year-old moccasin was buried under mountains of sheep dung and covered with ancient weeds. Cut from a single piece of leather and tanned with plant oils, the size 7 shoe was so well preserved that Zardaryan could see the impression of the wearer's big toe.

During the ten thousand years between sagebrush sandals and the first sneakers, unique shoes arose in every culture, from the simple *padukas* worn in ancient India to tiny Chinese lotus shoes designed for women who practiced ritual foot-binding. Ancient Egyptian pharaohs wore leather sandals embossed

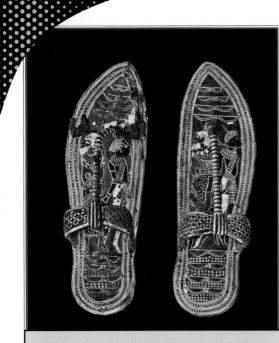

A pair of wooden sandals from the tomb of the ancient Egyptian pharaoh Tutankhamen is decorated in leather and gold leaf with images of enemy captives. Each sandal's sole shows a Nubian prisoner on the right and an Asiatic prisoner on the left.

with images of the slaves they dominated. Greek athletes in the ancient Olympic Games wore specialized sandals called *ligula*. Running shoes called *gallica* were developed in the Roman Empire.

And of course, fashionistas have always had their say. Style makers around the world embellished the basic shoe in countless weird and wonderful ways—heels and flats, buckles and bells, satin and fur.

From the Jungles of the New World

But what about sneakers?

These shoes didn't come from ancient Greece or the Roman Empire. In fact, the core component of the first sneakers—a rubber sole—originated in one of the least technologically advanced parts of the world, the Amazon Basin of South America. Indigenous peoples there had figured out how to tap hevea trees and use the milky latex sap to protect their feet from rocks, sticks, and biting insects. They poured hevea sap over foot-shaped lumps of hardened clay and then placed the sap-covered molds in the coals of a fire. In the hot smoke, the latex coagulated and stiffened into a crude rubber slipper, much like the modern Vibram FiveFingers shoes.

In the late 1700s, French and English travelers to the region brought back samples of the versatile goo, launching a "rubber fever" that swept through Europe and North America in the early 1800s. Manufacturing companies soon sprang up to produce this miracle material of the future on a grand scale. But the latex-smoking method of the Amazon peoples was not practical in North America. The material was too sticky in the heat and too brittle in the cold. It was useful for rubbing out pencil marks, which explains the name *rubber*, but not for much else. The new rubber companies went bankrupt, and most gave up on rubber.

Not Charles Goodyear.

Charles Goodyear, Dedicated Crackpot

The young American inventor was obsessed with rubber. Even when he was thrown in prison in the early 1800s for failing to pay his debts, he kept thinking about rubber. As soon as he was released, Goodyear went back to experimenting in his kitchen with stinky, oily batches of latex, trying to come up with a more long-lasting, durable substance.

Many people considered Goodyear to be a crackpot, bent over his stove, heating marshmallow-sized bits of latex on beds of sand, mixing the latex with everything from baby powder to magnesia. But he kept at it. One day he tried adding sulfur. A lump of the mixture flew out of his hands and landed on a piping hot woodstove nearby. He jumped to remove it, expecting the goo to melt and ruin the stove. Instead, it cooked solid, and when he pried it off, the material resembled leather. This accident proved to be a breakthrough—but not an instant success.

It took Goodyear decades of experimentation, several more trips to debtor's prison, and the ruination of his health to perfect the process of heating raw latex with sulfur—called vulcanization—and to create rubber as we know it. He envisioned a world where everything was made of rubber, from money and musical instruments to buildings and ships. Goodyear even wore rubber vests and used rubber calling cards.

But Goodyear was a terrible businessman. Rubber companies

pirated his technique and got rich off rubber. Charles Goodyear died in 1860, deeply in debt. His family never made any money from his discoveries and never had any part of the huge tire company named after him many years later.

Birth of the Plimsoll

Shortly after Goodyear's death, British and US rubber companies began producing shoes with rubber soles and lightweight cloth or leather uppers. These were the first sneakers. The new shoes were called sneaks and sneakers in the United States. In England they were called plimsolls because the seam between the upper part of the shoe and its sole reminded people of the marks painted onto the hulls of cargo ships. A Plimsoll line indicates the maximum depth at which a fully loaded cargo ship can safely travel and was named for British parliamentarian Samuel Plimsoll, who advocated for this safety protocol during the mid-1870s.

The new shoes grew in popularity, and by the late 1800s and early 1900s, most companies had their own line of rubber-soled shoes. In 1897 the Sears Roebuck & Company catalog was selling sneakers for sixty cents a pair. The New Liverpool Rubber Company developed specialized croquet shoes. The United States Rubber Company introduced Keds, a new brand of kids' shoes. Converse Rubber

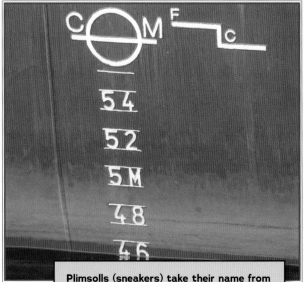

Plimsolls (sneakers) take their name from the Plimsoll line (*top*) on cargo ships.

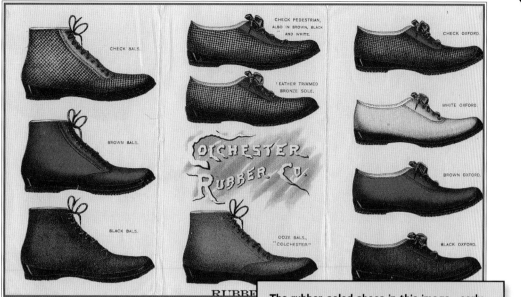

The rubber-soled shoes in this image—early forerunners of athletic shoes—were featured on the advertising pages of the Colchester Rubber Company's catalog around 1890.

Company hit the basketball courts with its famous high-tops. B. F. Goodrich patented a more comfortable insert for inside its sneakers called the Posture Foundation (PF) insole and launched a line of sneakers called PF Flyers, named after the technology.

Sneakers kept selling. Entrepreneurs saw opportunity and ran with it. By 1915 many of the important sneaker companies we know in the twenty-first century were already established. Bata Shoes started in Czechoslovakia. Joseph Foster launched the company that became Reebok. Brooks Sports and Hyde Athletic Industries, which is the parent company of Saucony and Spot-Bilt, were founded.

The sneaker century was off and running!

chapter 2

FROM FACTORIES TO RECREATIONAL SPORTS

When sneakers first hit the scene toward the end of the 1800s, working-class people in the United States and Great Britain wore lace-up leather shoes or heavy boots with leather soles. This was long-lasting footwear for hardworking citizens. Only the very wealthy had special shoes for dancing, parties, or posh athletic pursuits such as croquet and tennis.

Rubber-soled shoes are practical and functional. A book about female inmates in British prisons published in 1888 reported that "the night officer is generally accustomed to wear a species of India-rubber shoes or galoshes on her feet. These are termed 'sneaks' by the women [inmates]." The shoes also became associated with thieves because rubber soles made fast getaways possible. Kids started to wear sneakers because they were cheaper than leather shoes and fit their rough-and-tumble play.

By the early 1900s, basketball, baseball, football, and tennis were becoming increasingly popular in the United States. This was especially true among teenagers. Up until this time, most teens worked on the family farm or in the nation's factories, often dropping out of school by the age of thirteen. Laws eventually put limits on child labor and working hours, so kids were more likely to continue their education through high school. With the new labor laws, kids also had more leisure time, as did their parents. With more work-free hours every day, kids and adults devoted more time to sports. As more and more young people from diverse social and racial backgrounds began to attend high school, the importance of teenagers in the marketplace grew. Sneaker companies cast about for ways to reach this new group of consumers.

Athlete Ambassadors

The United States Rubber Company decided to target the youngest sneaker wearers. In 1916 the company focused production on one shoe—a simple, white, canvas lace-up with a blue rubber rectangle on the heel that said "Keds." This new brand name was a combination of the word *kid* and *ped*, a Latin root meaning "foot." Keds became the dominant brand in children's sneakers for decades.

Converse, an emerging sneaker company originally based in Malden, Massachusetts, realized that approaching young sneaker buyers through the sports they loved could be great for business. So, in 1917, they introduced a high-top canvas basketball sneaker called the All Star. Less than ten years later, pretty much every basketball player was wearing them, thanks to the work of a young player named Chuck Taylor.

Taylor started out as a high school basketball player in Columbus, Indiana. After graduating, he played semipro ball in the league that later became the NBA. Back then, basketball players didn't get paid much, so in 1921, Taylor became a salesman for Converse. He traveled the country, teaching basketball and promoting All Star athletic shoes. Along the way, he suggested improvements to the design of the shoe, including more traction, a stronger sole, and better ankle support.

By 1924 Taylor was considered the Ambassador of Basketball, and Converse had added his signature to the circular ankle patch on the All Star. After that, the shoes were usually called Chuck Taylors or simply Chucks. In many ways, the business relationship between Converse and Chuck Taylor was the first professional sports endorsement contract, and because of it, Converse had the jump on every other basketball shoe in the market—at least for a while.

B. F. Goodrich also wanted a well-known athlete to promote its sneakers. The company asked Canadian Jack Purcell, the 1933

Converse salesman extraordinaire Chuck Taylor keeps the ball away from his opponent on the court in 1921.

badminton champion of the world, to design a signature shoe for its line. His sneakers, now called Jack Purcells, look very similar to low-top Converse except for the black semicircle or "smile" on the toe caps.

The Keds, Chucks, and Jack Purcells designed in the 1920s and the 1930s delivered footwear that people wanted. In the twenty-first century, consumers can buy almost identical sneakers. The advantage to these relatively low-tech kicks is that they can be worn on the street just as easily as on a basketball court. But two of the biggest dogs in the sneaker industry—Adidas and NIKE, Inc.—got their start in a completely different way. They were racing to the top!

Chapter 3
RUNNING TOWARD GOLD

The human body is built for running. Around two million years ago, *Homo erectus*, a relative of modern humans, had developed the physical characteristics that make humans such incredible runners—long legs for long strides, butt muscles to stay upright, a unique piece of fibrous tissue known as the nuchal ligament to stabilize the head, brain-cooling features in the skull, and a foot stronger and more flexible than any architectural arch or suspension bridge.

Paleoanthropologists, the scientists who study early human ancestors, hypothesize that the evolution of the skeletons and musculature of early humans was driven by the need to chase down game for food. Even in the twenty-first century, the San people of the Kalahari, a desert in southern Africa, can run large antelope called kudu to the point of collapse, a form of hunting

At the 2008 Olympics, Puma's Complete Theseus II running shoes carried Jamaican sprinter Usain Bolt to victory in the 100-meter dash—even though one of his shoelaces was untied during the race. Bolt held onto the gold, winning the same race again in the 2012 Summer Olympics in London.

called persistence hunting. Lots of animals are faster than humans. But we're top of the heap, even in modern times—along with dogs, hyenas, and horses—when it comes to endurance running. For example, Kenyan Geoffrey Mutai ran the 2011 Boston Marathon in record time, 26.2 miles (42 kilometers) in just over two hours. In 2006 American ultramarathoner Dean Karnazes completed fifty marathons (1,310 miles, or 2,108 km) in fifty states in fifty days. Not that we're slackers in the speed department, either. In 2009 Jamaican sprinter Usain Bolt shattered the world record, clocking 100 meters in 9.58 seconds.

You Can't Outrun the Rarámuri

As a result of this human love of and talent for running, the biggest sneaker companies in the world started with track shoes. You might think it's surprising that multibillion-dollar companies were launched by such a simple sport. Running is low tech, requiring nothing more than the human body and the ground you race over. Truth is, you've probably never heard of the world's best runners, and they're not even wearing high-end sneakers.

The Tarahumara wear sandals made from old tires. This tribe, also called the Rarámuri or "running people," live in the Barrancas del Cobre (the Copper Canyons), a maze of treacherous, steep, cactus-covered crevasses slicing through the mountainous desert of central Mexico. It's easy for visitors to get lost or fall to their deaths there, but even Tarahumara grandmothers think nothing of running 50 miles (80 km) or even 100 miles (161 km) in a day. For fun, neighboring villages hold races that last two days and cover 300 miles (483 km). On the rare occasions when Tarahumara runners, wearing junky old sandals, have entered official competitions, they've left top runners eating dust and gasping for breath.

In some parts of the world, runners such as this young Kalenjin woman don't wear shoes while running.

On the other side of the world, in east-central Africa, the Kalenjin run barefoot. Members of this Kenyan ethnic group are built for efficient, long-distance speed. They're tall and slender, with long legs and short torsos. As children, they fly over the ground. As adults, they outperform the best professional competitors with only a few months of training. Unlike the Tarahumara, who rarely compete in official events, runners from Kenya have come to dominate long-distance races such as the Boston Marathon and track and field's 3,000-meter steeplechase, a cross-country race that involves leaping over barriers.

Olympic Glory

In 1896, when American and British kids were lacing up the earliest sneakers, top athletes gathered in Athens, Greece, for the first modern Olympic Games, inspired by similar contests in ancient Greece. Track-and-field events, especially the marathon, were highlights of the Games. Since then, the Summer Olympics have been the primary showcase for the remarkable human running machine and a place of innovation in the footwear department.

During the 1924 Summer Olympics in Paris, the British track-and-field team was wearing lightweight, hand-stitched leather shoes with metal spikes invented by British runner Joseph W. Foster in the 1890s. His company, J. W. Foster & Sons, later became the sneaker company Reebok, named after a type of speedy African antelope.

On the day of the 100-meter finals, British runner Harold Abrahams's nerves were on overdrive by the time he stepped up to the starting line. He'd botched the start during the semifinal but somehow managed to put on a superhuman burst of speed and qualify. Now, as he dug starting holes and secured the laces on his Fosters, he had a chance to be Britain's first champion in the 100-meter.

Abrahams was the underdog, but he was used to that. The Jewish runner said he had often felt bullied and alone in the face of anti-Semitism, both at his private high school and at Cambridge, where he had run on the college team. When the starting shot rang out, Abrahams's start was perfect and his speed electrifying. He finished in Olympic record time—10.52 seconds.

His victory and his shoes were immortalized in the 1981 movie *Chariots of Fire*, which won four Academy Awards, including one for costume design, thanks, in part, to the perfect replicas of the Foster's custom cleats Abrahams had raced in.

Under the Eyes of Hitler

At about the same time, a quiet young man in Germany named Adolf (Adi) Dassler was selling canvas slippers and leather dress shoes while tweaking designs for running shoes and soccer boots. His outgoing brother, Rudolf Dassler, ran the business side of the operation. In 1924 they launched a sports shoe company, Gebrüder Dassler, in Herzogenaurach, Germany.

Before long, the coach of Germany's Olympic track-and-field team was on the factory's doorstep, eager to discuss shoe design with Adi Dassler. The growing popularity of Adolf Hitler's National Socialist German Workers Party (the Nazi Party) was good business for the Dassler brothers. Hitler emphasized the importance of sports as a way to encourage patriotism, foster competitive drive, and increase physical fitness—all prerequisites for building an army to conquer Europe.

As the world boiled on the edge of war, the Dasslers churned out shoes.

In the run-up to the 1936 Summer Olympics, which would be held in Berlin, Germany, Hitler was adamant that the Games prove his belief that Caucasians were superior to all other races. He ordered the construction of a gigantic stadium and hired a filmmaker to document everything. Hitler planned to open the Games and be on hand to watch German athletes dominate event after event.

Most of the German runners were outfitted with Adi Dassler's handmade cleats, but Dassler cared far more about running than about Hitler's racial prejudices. He wanted to get his shoes on the feet of gifted African American runner Jesse Owens. As the Games got under way, Dassler searched the stadium and the

Olympic village, a pair of custom-made cleats in hand, looking for Owens. All he wanted was to convince the athlete to try them on. When he finally found Owens, Dassler made his request, and Owens took the shoes.

But would he wear them for his four events? Dassler had to wait to see. When the track-and-field events began, Owens took charge in the 100-meter race—10.3 seconds for the gold medal! But the next day, Owens fouled twice during the qualifying round for the long jump. Another foul and he'd be out of the running for that event's gold.

The Buckeye Bullet

James Cleveland Owens was born in Alabama in 1913. His family called him J. C., but when he moved to Ohio, the teacher at his new school mispronounced it and called him Jesse. The name stuck. When he started winning races, first in high school and later at Ohio State University (OSU), fans gave him another nickname, the Buckeye Bullet. While studying at OSU, Owens worked multiple jobs to support himself and his wife, Ruth. He pumped gas, waited tables, and shelved books in the library.

Somehow he still found the energy to train, drawing on his ability to power through tough situations. In the lead-up to the Berlin Olympics, Owens was scheduled to compete in the 1935 Big Ten Championships. Hours before the events began, Owens hurt his back falling down a flight of stairs. It could've been the end of a promising career. Instead, he ran the 100-yard (91.4 m) sprint in 9.4 seconds, tying the world record, and broke world records in three other events.

After his stunning success at the Olympics, Owens traveled the United States, speaking at youth groups, civic meetings, and schools. In 1976 US president Gerald Ford awarded him the Presidential Medal of Freedom, the highest possible civilian honor.

Innovations

Adi Dassler never stopped fiddling with sneaker design. He registered many patents for innovations large and small. Among the most important was his development of screw-in, interchangeable spikes for the soles of sneakers, an invention that led to Adidas's decades-long domination of the soccer sport shoe market.

Dassler's moment of triumph came at the final game of the 1954 World Cup in Bern, Switzerland. The German soccer team was the underdog, barely scraping its way into the championship match against Hungary's Mighty Magyars, a team undefeated in international competition for the previous four years. By halftime, the Germans had managed to even the score to 2–2, but a torrential rainstorm was turning the field to mud. Dassler was on the sidelines, ready

Adidas founder Adolf (Adi) Dassler screws studs into soccer cleats on November 30, 1954. The following day, Germany's national soccer team would wear Dassler's customized soccer shoes in a match against England.

to dive into action, when the coach of the German team gave the order to deploy the new spikes. Quickly, Dassler and the players swapped out the shorter, grass-gripping spikes for Dassler's longer spikes, designed to provide traction in slippery conditions. The technology gave the players the edge they needed to hang on. Five minutes before the end of the game, striker Helmut Rahn nailed the ball and sealed a 3–2 victory for Germany.

The unlikely triumph was called *Das Wunder von Bern*, the "Miracle of Bern." It was a miracle for Adidas as well. The company launched a print advertising campaign for the winning soccer boots, and countries around the world began knocking on Adi Dassler's door to outfit their soccer teams. Adidas's dominance in soccer gear continues into the twenty-first century. The company was a primary sponsor of the 2014 World Cup and created the event's signature ball, the Brazuca.

This time, he nailed it. In the long jump finals, Owens sailed 8.06 meters (26.4 feet), winning gold and beating the former world record by 6 inches (15.2 centimeters). In front of the world, German long jumper and second-place finisher Luz Long embraced Jesse Owens, and together they acknowledged the cheering crowd.

In the next few days, Owens went on to win two more gold medals. He set world records in both the 200-meter and the 4x100-meter relay and became the first American to win four Olympic gold medals in track and field in a single Games.

And that hug? It made history.

Luz Long was Hitler's perfect example of white superiority. Owens was the grandson of an Alabama slave. Yet both were athletes striving for excellence and gracious sportsmen who respected each other. Still, at the medal ceremony, the contrast couldn't have been greater, with Long giving the Nazi salute and Owens saluting the American flag. And on Owens's feet? A pair of sleek, brown spikes with Adi Dassler's signature stripes.

At the 1936 Olympic medal ceremony, gold medalist Jesse Owens (*center*) saluted the United States while German silver medalist Luz Long (*right*) gave the Nazi salute. Despite political differences, Owens wore German-made track shoes.

Battle of the Brothers

Across lines of nationality, religion, and race, the love of sport had united Adi Dassler, Luz Long, and Jesse Owens at the 1936 Olympic Games. But on the eve of World War II (1939–1945), American and European shoe companies were in trouble. They lost workers to the military, struggled to find raw materials, and were forced to repurpose their factories to make uniforms and other supplies to support the war effort. In the United States, Converse produced flying boots for the US Army Air Corps. Gola, a top producer of British soccer shoes, switched to army boots. Shoemaking stopped altogether at Gebrüder Dassler when the factory was ordered to weld parts for German Panzer tanks.

Wartime tensions rose between the Dassler brothers. Adi wanted only to tinker with shoe designs, while Rudolf was strident in his support of Hitler's policies. For Adi, who thought his brother was a loudmouthed braggart, pleasing the Nazis was an unpleasant necessity of doing business. The breaking point came when Rudolf was drafted into the German army, while Adi was left in charge of Gebrüder Dassler. Adi's role running all operations at the factory was considered too crucial to send him to the front lines. The enmity between the brothers was so great that Rudolf was convinced his brother had plotted to send him to his death.

The war ended in 1945 with Germany's defeat. When American tanks rolled to a stop in front of the Gebrüder Dassler factory that year, Adi's charming wife, Käthe, saved it from destruction by convincing the soldiers that all the company wanted to do was make sports shoes. What could be less threatening than that?

The factory went back into the civilian shoe business, but the brothers never made peace. They split the business in 1948. Adi Dassler called his new company Adidas. He developed the signature three-stripe design in blazing white on the side of the shoe to ensure that everyone recognized his work. Rudolf Dassler founded Puma, with the distinctive downward curving formstripe—also white and easy to see—on the side of the shoes. These two men, their companies, and their families were rivals for decades. Their battles for economic supremacy were fought during the track-and-field events of the Olympic Games, where the shoes on the athletes' feet became as important as clocking the fastest time.

Chapter 4
GETTING OFF ON THE RIGHT FOOT

In the 1950s, after the Allied victory in World War II, Americans entered a period of booming economic prosperity. In that era, a quirky, absentminded teenager named Phil Knight was an honor roll student and middle-distance runner at Cleveland High School in Portland, Oregon. After graduation he went to the University of Oregon and joined the track team. He wasn't a superstar, but his coach, the demanding, obsessive Bill Bowerman, thought he was a solid middle-distance runner. At the university, he ran with the best of the best on Hayward Field, a track known for producing top finishers.

After college Knight went to Stanford Business School in California, where an assignment to write about small businesses got him thinking about track and field again. He was passionate about the sport, but was there any money to be made in it? At first glance, you didn't need much more than a T-shirt, shorts, and a pair of shoes to hit the road.

Still, if Knight had learned one thing from Bowerman, it was this: the top runners were wearing running shoes manufactured by Adidas, and even those weren't good enough. At the University of Oregon, Knight had watched Bowerman modify existing cleats and even custom-make shoes for his athletes. Knight recognized that making better shoes—and having the personal connections to get the new gear to promising runners—could be the foundation for a killer business.

For his class assignment, Knight worked up a plan for a US-based shoe company that would distribute made-in-Japan sneakers to high school and college athletes. Knight focused on Japan because labor was cheap there. By producing good athletic shoes at a lower cost, his imaginary company could undercut Adidas's prices, especially if a sales force could take advantage of Knight's friendship with Bowerman and reach out to other coaches. It seemed plausible that Knight's small-business plan could actually work. He turned in the assignment and moved on to other things.

In 1962 Knight graduated from Stanford, bombed his first job interview, and decided to travel the world before getting serious about work again. On a whim, he ended up in Japan, where he found knockoff Adidas shoes for sale. The shoes, complete with the classic three-stripe logo, had been pirated by a company called Onitsuka Tiger. Knight decided to pay the company a visit.

Ushered into an impromptu meeting with several Onitsuka Tiger representatives, Knight made up a name for his pretend company on the spot. He called it Blue Ribbon Sports. When he walked out of the meeting, he had convinced Onitsuka Tiger that he was a US shoe distributor with cash to place an order. Later, he scribbled in his notebook, "Faked out Tiger Shoe Co" and dug out his old business plan assignment determined to make it a reality. He had to borrow thirty-seven dollars from his dad to order sample shoes.

It took a while for Knight to hammer out a distribution deal with Onitsuka Tiger (which became Asics in 1977). But as soon as he had his order of Tiger sneakers in hand, he made his first sales pitch to his former coach, Bill Bowerman. Knight was hoping that Bowerman would order some shoes or at least recommend them to fellow coaches. He was shocked when Bowerman proposed a partnership. Knight would handle the financial side of the business. Bowerman would help design new styles and recommend them to college track teams across the United States. Knight and Bowerman each agreed to contribute $500, and in 1964, with a handshake, the company that would become NIKE, Inc., was born.

Sneakers Off Track

Phil Knight's timing couldn't have been better. Something curious was happening in the United States. Sneakers were sneaking up on everyone in the 1960s. An article in the *New Yorker* magazine observed that "a revolution . . . seems to be taking place in footgear." The "once lowly sneaker" was selling 150 million pairs a year. What was going on?

The decades after World War II were a golden age for teenagers. They had more free time and more spending money than ever before. Thanks to movies and the arrival of television, they also had a window into a wider world. Wearing sneakers outside of the basketball court was a way to make a statement, to rebel against parents, and to shun old-school ways. Simple sneakers—a little canvas, a little rubber—were making huge inroads by capturing cool.

Counterculture movie-star icon James Dean was photographed on the set of the 1955 movie *Rebel Without a Cause*—a story

The tough-talking, street-smart gangs of 1961's movie musical *West Side Story* faced off while wearing rival shoe brands. Here, the Jets and their white Keds surround a member of the Sharks (*far left*), clad in black Chucks.

of teen love, rebellion, and drag racing—wearing a pair of Jack Purcells. The 1961 movie musical *West Side Story* told a version of the classic Romeo and Juliet story but was set in ethnically divided New York City. Careful costuming separated the slick style of two battling gangs. The all-white Polish American Jets wore white Keds, and the Puerto Rican Sharks fought in black, low-top Chucks. Sneakers became associated with action heroes such as Steve McQueen, the star of *The Great Escape*, a popular 1963 film about American prisoners of war during World War II. A photo shoot by *Life* magazine that year shows ultracool McQueen in a pair of plain white sneakers.

Appealing to a younger audience, Walt Disney Studios spread sneaker fever too. In *The Absent-Minded Professor* (1961), a goofy science teacher invents a substance called flubber. When he adds this "flying rubber" to the soles of the local basketball team's sneakers, the players make soaring leaps and dominate the game. *The Computer Wore Tennis Shoes* (1969), in which an electrical shock turns the brain of a school troublemaker into a computer, also capitalized on the sneaker trend.

Courting Top Athletes

Meanwhile, back on the track, Adidas was running laps around Puma. By 1960 almost all top Olympic track-and-field athletes were wearing Adidas three-stripes. Adi Dassler's sixteen Adidas factories were churning out twenty-two thousand pairs of shoes a day. He was outselling Puma nine to one. Rudolf Dassler and the team at Puma had to find some way to break the Adidas stranglehold.

Shoe companies paid close attention to the ultra-swift feet of American runner Wilma Rudolph. Here, she races to victory in the 100-meter dash at the 1960 Olympics in Rome—in Adidas shoes.

Puma needed to get formstripes on someone like Wilma Rudolph, a lanky runner from Tennessee, who became an Olympic superstar at the 1960 Summer Games in Rome, Italy. Watching her eat up the track, many people found it hard to believe that Rudolph had been a sickly child, never expected to walk well, much less run, after bouts with scarlet fever, double pneumonia, whooping cough, measles, and polio. In Rome Rudolph won gold medals in the 100-meter, the 200-meter, and the 4x100-meter relay—all in Adidas.

Another star of the Rome Olympics was Ethiopian runner Abebe Bikila. An Adidas representative got Bikila into a pair of running shoes for the Games, but a few days before the race, his new shoes gave him a blister. At the starting line, Bikila took off the uncomfortable shoes. He ran the marathon's 26.2 miles (42.2 km) in two hours, fifteen minutes, and sixteen seconds, winning gold. And he did it all barefoot! Four years later, Bikila won the Olympic marathon in Tokyo, Japan—this time wearing Pumas.

Dirty Dealings

An ambitious German sprinter named Armin Hary, who had worn Adidas shoes for years, decided to take advantage of the Adidas–Puma rivalry. Before the 1960 Summer Games in Rome, he approached a company representative to ask just how much Adidas would be willing to pay if he were to promise to wear their spikes in his races. At the time, it was a shocking request. Olympic athletes were strictly forbidden from being paid to train and from accepting commercial endorsements. Athletes usually chose the shoes they liked best, not the ones that could make them the most money.

Adidas refused the deal. So Hary went to lunch with Puma.

In the final for the 100-meter sprint, Hary raced to gold, flashing the Puma formstripe. Puma had agreed to pay him 10,000 Deutsche (German) Marks (US $2,400) to wear the shoes. The Adidas clan was stunned, but at the medals ceremony, Puma's jubilation collapsed. Hary had switched into Adidas cleats for the ceremony, hoping to get money from both sides of the sneaker war. The ploy backfired. Adidas refused to have anything more to do with the sprinter. But Hary's under-the-table deals changed sports forever.

Four years later, the Summer Olympics in Tokyo, Japan, were like a spy novel come to life. To work around the Olympic rules against endorsements, athletes and shoe company representatives would rendezvous in Olympic Village bathrooms.

The sneaker reps would leave envelopes of money in the stalls and then disappear. The athletes would compare how much Adidas, Puma, and Onitsuka Tiger had left and then give their loyalty to the highest bidder.

As secret, illegal payments were becoming the new name of the game at the 1964 Olympics, Phil Knight and Bill Bowerman were back in the United States, launching their little sneaker company. Over time, NIKE, Inc., would come to understand better than any other company how to use athlete and pop-star endorsements to dominate the sneaker market.

Waffles for Everyone

NIKE founder Phil Knight always dreamed big. Even with Adidas-wearing athletes dominating the medals ceremonies in Tokyo, Knight fully intended to take down the German shoe company. Jeff Johnson, the company's first full-time salesperson, logged thousands of miles selling Blue Ribbon sneakers out of the trunk of his car on college campuses and high school tracks up and down the West Coast of the United States.

As Knight struggled to maintain the often rocky relationship with Onitsuka Tiger, Bill Bowerman kept searching for ways to improve the sneakers his athletes wore for racing. What about improvements to running spikes? Could they be made of rubber? Would a different shape increase the shoe's traction?

While making waffles one morning, Bowerman was struck by inspiration. He looked at the square depressions in the waffle iron and promptly ditched the waffle batter for liquid urethane. He poured the stinky stuff into the waffle iron and . . .

Oops!

Bowerman had forgotten to add a secondary chemical that allowed the mixture to harden so it would easily release from the mold. The waffle iron was ruined, but the idea had legs.

Bowerman's "waffle soles" provided extra traction, especially on Astroturf. Manufacturers incorporated the new soles into football shoes and sneakers, which the company sold as Moon Shoes.

A Victory Swoosh

With the company changing fast, Knight and Bowerman wanted to focus on their own designs and break free of Onitsuka Tiger. They needed a new name and their very own set of stripes. Jeff Johnson proposed a name: Nike, the Greek goddess of victory. Knight asked Carolyn Davidson, an art student in Portland, Oregon, to design a logo. He asked her to sketch something that captured movement and speed. She came back with a curvy checkmark. Nobody liked it, but they were pressed for time and out of options, so they accepted the design. At the time, Knight paid Davidson $35 for the logo. In 1983 he compensated her with five hundred shares of NIKE stock, worth well over $500,000 by 2014. The swoosh has since become the most recognized brand image in the world.

Stripes: Know Your Shoe

Whether they are straight or curved, lines or swooshes, the brand-distinguishing colored bits of fabric or leather on the sides of sneakers are called stripes. In the earliest running shoes, these strips of leather served a functional purpose. They added structure to the sides of the shoes and extra support to the foot inside.

When the Dassler brothers split their shoe empire in 1948, they wanted to separate their brands visually. Stripes were an eye-catching way to do that. In the twenty-first century, the stripes still add support in some models, but their primary job is to make sure you know exactly what kind of sneaker you're looking at.

Riding the Jogging Boom

Even with a fancy new swoosh, NIKE couldn't hope to topple Adidas unless the company expanded sales beyond elite athletes. To dominate the world sneaker market, NIKE had to bring the sneakers to the masses.

At about this time, Bowerman became interested in a new exercise craze called jogging. The idea was simple and had nothing to do with winning races. Regular people, from middle-aged moms to overweight dads, could participate. All they had to do was trot along at a slow, regular pace. In a 1967 book titled *Jogging: A Physical Fitness Program for All Ages*, Bowerman and his coauthor, Dr. Waldo Harris, told readers that jogging was the key to health.

Suddenly suburban Americans were buying sneakers and jogging through their neighborhoods. By the late 1970s, one report estimated that 48 percent of adults in the United States had tried jogging. Registrations in the New York Marathon had risen from 156 runners in 1970 to 5,000 in 1977. Nike swooshes were on most of those feet.

These sneakers weren't the formfitting, lightweight, spiked shoes

During the 1970s, jogging became a popular pastime for people all around the United States. Shoe manufacturers paid attention, developing a wider range of sneakers, especially for women.

from the track. They were brightly colored waffle trainers with knobbly treads, arch supports, nylon uppers, and foam cushion soles. Riding the jogging boom, NIKE shouldered Adidas out of the way and began its rise to top-dog position in the sneaker business. But the company missed the boat on the next fitness fad.

Life Is Not a Spectator Sport

By the 1980s, aerobics had taken center stage. The fast-paced workout classes included dance-like moves set to music and were led by perky, enthusiastic instructors. Almost all participants were women, a group of sneaker consumers that NIKE, with its all-male management team, didn't understand very well. But Paul Fireman, the leader of Reebok, went on instinct and decided to throw his resources into making sneakers specifically for women.

Reebok Freestyles, released in 1982, were exactly what many women were looking for—lightweight, ultrasoft, and flattering. In other words, they were everything many women thought NIKE's waffle trainers were not. Women wore Reeboks for aerobics and kept on wearing them to the store, to work, and around the house.

Popular actress Cybill Shepherd wore a pair of bright orange Freestyles with a long black gown to the televised Emmy Awards in 1985. Supermodel Cindy Crawford wore Reeboks in her popular exercise videos. Singer Paula Abdul belted out her 1988 pop hit "Straight Up" in television commercials for the shoes. As the song's lyrics implied, Reebok was definitely having fun.

After the introduction of the Freestyle, Reebok's yearly sales jumped from $3.5 million to $13 million. By 1986 annual sales had skyrocketed to $841 million, while NIKE's sales had fallen to $536 million. Reebok had surpassed the biggest US sneaker brand because it realized that sneakers weren't running shoes or jogging shoes or aerobics shoes. They were simply shoes. In fact, by the end of the 1980s, 80 percent of sneaker wearers weren't participating in sports of any kind. Sneakers had become part of everyday life.

The 1982 National Collegiate Athletic Association (NCAA) Division 1 Championship game pitted the Georgetown Hoyas against the University of North Carolina Tar Heels. With less than two minutes to go, Sleepy Floyd scored for Georgetown, putting his basketball team on top 62–61. After a timeout, play resumed against the backdrop of a screaming crowd.

North Carolina's top players, James Worthy and Sam Perkins, were blocked at every turn. But coach Dean Smith had a brilliant plan up his sleeve—get the ball to nineteen-year-old freshman guard Michael Jordan. Seventeen seconds before the buzzer, Michael Jordan had one of those moments that changes everything. He flew across the left wing to score the winning point for North Carolina. The crowd exploded. What Michael Jordan didn't know was that, even then, NIKE had its eye on him.

To respond to fierce competition in the athletic shoe market, NIKE's strategy was changing. The company wanted a single athlete around whom they could build a bigger-than-life persona. In Jordan, NIKE saw extraordinary talent and confident style. He had the makings of a hero. The problem? Jordan was an Adidas man through and through. As a Tar Heel, he suited up in Converse, but off-court it was all three-stripes. NIKE had some convincing to do.

In 1984 Jordan decided to go professional and was selected as the No. 3 NBA draft pick by the Chicago Bulls. His $3 million, five-year contract with the Bulls was the third highest ever for a rookie. He won Olympic gold with the US basketball team that same summer in Los Angeles.

NIKE turned up the heat, offering Jordan a $2.5 million endorsement deal, the largest basketball endorsement of the time. Jordan said yes, and from there NIKE created an entire Michael Jordan world—signature shoes, a clothing line, his own logo, and dedicated print and video advertising. The Air Jordan 1 shoe paired newly designed air soles with a winged basketball logo and Chicago Bulls colors—red and black. Ads on television featured Jordan in midair on his way to a slam dunk with the voice-over, "Who says man was not meant to fly?"

In 1985 the NBA banned the Air Jordan 1 from the court because the shoes were not the officially approved NBA colors. Jordan wore them anyway and was fined $1,000. NIKE whipped out an ad that showed a defiant Jordan with blacked-out shoes. Jordan's boldness sent shoe sales through the roof. Fans were falling over one another to pay $65 a pair for Air Jordans, even though they were the most expensive basketball shoe at the time. The shoes made $130 million for NIKE in the first year of sales.

Michael Jordan became a larger-than-life icon for teens across the country. He was especially popular among urban African Americans, many of whom viewed basketball as a way out of inner-city poverty and into fame and fortune. Wearing Air Jordans became a way to make a statement about fashion and aspiration, determination and defiance.

Rocking the Beat

Basketball wasn't the only thing inspiring urban teens of the 1980s. About the same time Michael Jordan signed with NIKE, a new genre of music was emerging. Born in New York's South Bronx, rap music was the product of urban street culture. Driving beats, spoken lyrics, and mash-up sampling powered the music. DJs reigned over the growing hip-hop scene.

Three guys from Queens, New York, who called themselves Run-D.M.C. took rap music mainstream when their album, also called *Run-D.M.C.*, went gold in 1984, selling more than five hundred thousand copies. Along with the music came a unique urban style— fedora hats, track suits, gold chains, and unlaced sneakers.

Which sneakers?

Run-D.M.C. was 100 percent Adidas, and their 1986 hit song "My Adidas" immortalized the white shell toes the group wore onstage.

The members of the hip-hop group Run-D.M.C. took pride in their Adidas sneakers as well as in their pioneering beats. Fans rushed to copy the rappers' fashion sense, and Adidas sales soared.

Adidas saw an opportunity to interact directly with a powerful new urban market. The company quickly brought an endorsement deal to Run-D.M.C. It didn't take long for other sneaker companies to get smart. Celebrities outside the sporting world could sell shoes too. In the twenty-first century, it seems that every megastar, from Jay-Z to Justin Bieber to Nicki Minaj, has a sneaker line, but it was a revolutionary idea in the 1980s.

Timing turned out to be as important as signing big stars to endorse athletic shoes. For example, the dominant pop star of the 1980s was Michael Jackson. Everyone wanted to do his

Fast Times, Vans, and Product Placement

In the 1982 movie *Fast Times at Ridgemont High*, bad-boy actor Sean Penn tumbles out of a VW bus wearing black-and-white checkered slip-ons called Vans. The laceless sneakers were originally designed as deck shoes for sailors and were adopted in the 1960s by skaters and surfers as their shoe of choice. The movie catapulted Vans into popularity. The resulting sales flurry caught the company off guard. No one in management at Vans even knew the film's costume department had used the shoes in the movie.

Using a particular brand of a product in a movie is known as product placement. Companies can pay to have their products featured prominently in a movie or on a TV show, and the practice has become widespread. For example, if you pay attention, you'll notice that bad guy Aleksei Sytsevich in *The Amazing Spider-Man 2* (2014) wears an Adidas sweat suit.

Typically, real products show up in films, but figments of a moviemaker's imagination can become actual products as well. The glowing Nikes that Marty McFly wears in *Back to the Future II* (1989) started out as movie fun, but in 2011, NIKE issued a limited-release replica. The Mag Air, without the self-tying laces, has since sold for more than $37,000 a pair on eBay. In the future, we may actually get sneakers with a self-tightening feature, according to NIKE designer Tinker Hatfield.

signature dance move, the moonwalk. His glittering single glove and red leather jacket were unmistakable. In 1990 LA Gear signed Jackson to design a line of athletic shoes and clothes as part of a campaign dubbed "Unstoppable." But by this point, Jackson's fame was waning, and the buckle-covered black sneakers he designed didn't sell well. LA Gear learned an expensive lesson in timing.

Meanwhile, sneakers kept showing up at the movies. A character in Spike Lee's 1989 film *Do the Right Thing* nearly comes to blows with a neighbor who has scuffed his brand-new Air Jordans. The movie, about racial tensions in a Brooklyn neighborhood, cemented Lee's reputation as a director who gave voice to urban youth. He was so popular that NIKE hired Lee to do a series of Air Jordan commercials.

Urban street culture—music, dance, clothes, shoes, and sports heroes—spread to suburban white America and into high fashion. Suddenly, African American teens in the roughest neighborhoods of the country's biggest cities were the style makers.

Opportunity or Exploitation?

To see if new styles would fly with the kids who mattered, shoe designers took new models into inner-city neighborhoods of major US cities, offering them for free at parks and playgrounds. Known as bro-ing, the method was a great way to get feedback on the new styles from communities that would eventually buy them.

Once NIKE zeroed in on the newest, hippest shoes, the company fed the frenzy by producing new models in limited quantities and releasing them for sale at well-hyped events. Massive crowds gathered at sneaker stores, often becoming pushy and aggressive as eager buyers fought to be the first ones in the door to buy the newest Air Jordans.

Prices rose from $65 a pair to well over $100, even though many sneaker fans had little money to spare. Shoe thefts began

Bro-ing

NIKE grabbed its in-the-streets market research technique from the ski industry. A "pro-deal," or "pro-ing," meant letting top skiers test out new skis for free. The sneaker version, known as "bro-ing," was conducted by NIKE employees who offered free shoes to inner-city kids with some version of the question, Hey brother, want to check out some shoes?

to increase, as did shoe-related violence. Police departments in big cities reported more and more sportswear-related crimes. In one highly publicized case, a fifteen-year-old boy in Fort Meade, Maryland, was killed by a friend for his sneakers. In addition, urban gangs were beginning to adopt particular shoe brands, such as Adidas, and other branded sportswear.

The aggressive marketing by sneaker companies in the inner city created such an unquenchable demand that many desperately poor young people were forgoing food in favor of saving money for sneaks. They were braving the trampling crowds at shoe releases and then risking their lives wearing them on the street. In response to these trends, African American politician and civil rights leader Jesse Jackson criticized sneaker companies for exploiting urban teens. Operation PUSH, a Chicago-based organization he founded to promote civil rights and social justice, urged a boycott. NIKE was the primary target because it dominated most of the sneaker market, had no African Americans in important positions within the company, and specifically targeted seductive advertising at the teens least able to afford the company's shoes.

The boycott never took off. Teens didn't abandon their kicks, and sneaker companies didn't stop making money off of them. By the end of the 1980s, sneaker sales had risen to $12 billion, doubling in less than ten years. Epic profits for sneaker companies have continued to rise ever since.

Big Money

How big is the money? Extraordinarily big.

In 2014 the global footwear market was valued at almost $80 billion. NIKE, Inc., commands about 20 percent of the market, and the majority of NIKE's profits come from the semi-independent Jordan brand. Basketball shoes drive the industry. The LeBron X+, released in 2012, is top of the line. The shoe is equipped with Nike+ technology to allow wearers to track how high they jump, how fast they run, and how hard they play. After practice, wearers can then share performance stats on a worldwide social network dedicated to sports. Sounds pretty sweet, but you'll pay for the technology. The shoe carried a price tag of almost $300 a pair.

The Nike Air Yeezy II, designed by rapper Kanye West and released in 2012, retailed for $250 a pair but went as high as $89,000 for a single pair in presales on eBay. The shoe, named for Kanye's nickname, Yeezy, has uppers made of anaconda-textured leather in various colors, a ridged strip down the heel, and glow-in-the-dark soles.

These may be the sneakers of the future, but most teens can't afford them. D'Wayne Edwards, a former Air Jordan designer, says, "Kids created the monster the industry is today, but the companies haven't done anything for them." The social and political issues of the 1990s continued to plague the sneaker industry into the twenty-first century.

Kanye West is no stranger to the sneaker world. He designed his first sneaker collection in 2009 for French designer Louis Vuitton. That collection included the $800 red Yeezys shown here, which West later claimed had been overpriced.

Women Got Game

While male athletes are raking in the cash, few female athletes have been offered big endorsement deals. The top three female earners in 2013 were all tennis players. Russian-born pro Maria Sharapova pulled in $29 million in prize money, appearance fees, and endorsement deals with NIKE, Head, and other, non-sportswear companies. American legend Serena Williams made $20.5 million, including $12 million from deals with NIKE and Wilson. Li Na, from China, earned $18.2 million. Her primary sponsors are Samsung and Mercedes-Benz, not sneaker companies. It's good money, but not anywhere close to the $78 million Tiger Woods scored during the same time period.

What will it take for women athletes to wield the same influence as male sports icons?

Maya Moore, the most valuable player in the 2013 Women's National Basketball Association (WNBA) Championship Finals, may be the game changer. In May 2011, the Minnesota Lynx player became the first woman to sign an endorsement deal with the Jordan brand. Her player exclusive Air Jordan XX3s—released in 2013—are sleek turquoise and cobalt high-tops.

The brand is focusing on Moore's athleticism and dedication to basketball, a shift from endorsement spots that have focused on the sex appeal of female athletes. As women's sports gain momentum—and, more important, a growing fan base—you can expect to see more big deals for women like Moore.

Tennis star Maria Sharapova competes at the 2013 French Open wearing a customized pair of Nikes (Zoom Vapor 9 Tour iD). Sharapova's sponsorship agreement with NIKE, Inc., earns her millions of dollars in exchange for promoting the company's fancy footwear.

Chapter 6
SNEAKERS AND THE GLOBAL ECONOMY

Sneakers have come a long way since Adi Dassler and Bill Bowerman were hand-stitching custom shoes for runners. The sneakers you're wearing today traveled around the world and passed through hundreds of hands before they got to your feet. In fact, sneakers are the poster child for the dominant economic trend of the last three decades—globalization. Follow a sneaker, and you'll see the world.

Design = Vision + Materials

Each shoe begins with the artistic vision of a designer. This person, usually working in the sneaker company's home country, dreams up the look of the shoe. The pressure is on to be creative because new sneaker models are introduced every week. Sometimes a celebrity collaborates with the design team

Around the world

The big dogs in the sneaker industry tend to dominate the story of sneakers. NIKE, Adidas (now including Reebok), Puma, and Asics claim more than 30 percent of the sneaker market. But there are lots of less well-known companies creating distinctive kicks. Here are just a few of them:

- Babolat, a French company founded in 1875, focuses on shoes for tennis, badminton, and padel, a paddle sport popular in Spain and Latin America.
- New Balance, founded in 1906, is dedicated to the happiness of runners.
- Etnies, a favorite brand for skateboarders and BMXers, was founded in 1986 by a French skater living in California.
- Li-Ning is a booming Chinese sneaker company, launched in 1990, which may soon cross swords with the biggies.
- Visvim shoes are proudly alternative. The Japanese company, founded in 2001, makes brightly colored moccasin sneaks.
- Blackspot came on the scene in 2004, bucking the trend of large, highly visible brand symbols such as sneaker stripes by refusing to use trademarks.
- White Mountaineering, a Japanese company founded in 2006, makes athletic shoes with an outdoorsy vibe.
- Android Homme and its preeminent brand, Propulsion Hi, launched in 2008 with upscale sneaks popular with musicians such as Justin Bieber and Usher.

to create a specialty shoe for the brand. After the new sneaker is sketched out, a developer and a team of technicians make a prototype.

Materials are sourced from around the world and make up about 12 percent of the shoe's sticker price. If the upper is leather, then a ranch in Venezuela may provide the cowhide, which might be tanned in a facility in South Korea. The outer soles of early model sneakers were made of hevea rubber from Brazil or Indonesia. In the twenty-first century, outer soles are made of high-tech materials such as synthetic rubber from Taiwan.

The midsole, the thick cushioning layer sandwiched between the tread on the bottom of the shoe and the innersole, has a huge effect on sneaker performance. For this reason, many technological innovations are developed for the midsole. Most companies use ethylene vinyl acetate (EVA), a plastic foam rubber often made in South Korea, for this part of the shoe. If the sneaker is a Nike Air model, the midsole includes an airbag cushioning system developed in 1979 and manufactured in the United States. By keeping this part of the production in the United States, the company can keep an eye on the top-secret technology.

New innovations are coming fast. In 2013 Adidas introduced the brand-new Boost sole technology, a layer of fused plastic pellets made of thermoplastic polyurethane (TPU) for added cushioning. NIKE is using 3-D printers to fabricate running cleats.

Ostrich and Stingray Skin

Singer Beyoncé had a vision for a pair of custom kicks for herself to be modeled after the high-heel wedge sneakers created in 2012 by French designer Isabel Marant. In 2013 Beyoncé got a sneaker customizer called Perfectly Made Kicks (PMK) to remake the shoe in ostrich, stingray, crocodile, anaconda, and calf skins, provoking the outrage of People for the Ethical Treatment of Animals (PETA).

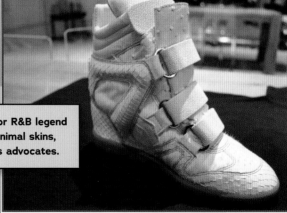

The King Bey sneaker, customized for R&B legend Beyoncé to feature various exotic animal skins, ruffled feathers among animal rights advocates.

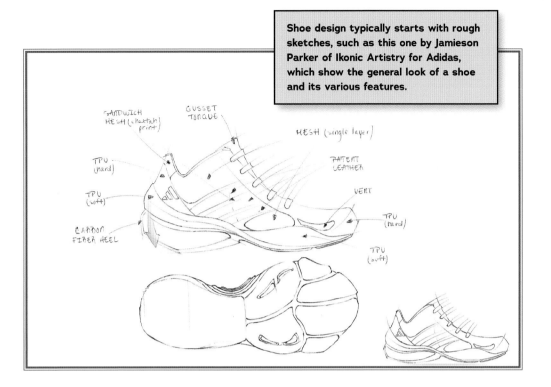

Designed in collaboration with gold medal sprinter Michael Johnson, the Vapor HyperAgility cleats are designed to enhance speed and may look to the untrained eye like something grown in an alien lab.

Build Me a Shoe

Making sneakers is very labor intensive. Automated sewing machines are able to sew flat things together, but a sneaker has a complicated, three-dimensional shape that requires joining and bending fabric edges that are then stitched together. As a result, every sneaker is assembled almost completely by hand. While New Balance and Vans still produce some Made in America sneakers, most brands are manufactured in China, Indonesia, or Vietnam.

From eyelet to tongue to toe cap to sole, putting together a sneaker is no small task. All the pieces, more than fifty in most models, start out flat as pancakes. One by one, these pieces are hand assembled by as many as 120 shoe factory workers, each doing one specific part of the process. "This is a precision job!" explains sneaker engineering technician Eric Graham. "Skilled stitchers are needed for the majority of the construction [and] for the majority of shoe models."

First, lining material is sewn to the upper body of the shoe, which is made of fabric or leather. The upper body of the shoe is stitched up the back. Plastic or fabric toe-and-heel reinforcers are then heat molded into the flexible shell of the sneaker. At this stage, logos, embroidery, and embellishments are added. The next step is to sew on a rigid innersole of foam, cloth, or cardboard. For shoes designed to work with interactive, performance-tracking technology, a slot in the midsole, under the sock liner, holds the tracking device.

It's time to put the rest of the sole together. Two pieces, the midsole and the outsole, are cleaned, primed, and coated with a liquid adhesive. This stinky, thick, honey-like glue is applied with small brushes. The midsole and the outsole are then heated to 212°F (100°C) to make the adhesive very sticky. When the pieces come out of the oven, the shoe assembler has sixty seconds to fit the two layers of the sole together perfectly. The worker quickly puts the sole under pressure with a weighted last (a foot-shaped form) so the glue will cross-link, in the same way Velcro fibers come together.

Finally, it's time to put the sneaker together. The upper is laced onto the last, and the assembler draws a bite line to show exactly where the edge of the sole should hit the upper. Next, the worker applies a layer of adhesive to the top of the sole and the bottom of the upper. Both pieces make another trip through the hot oven. Hand assembly begins at the toe, moves to the heel, and completes in the middle. If the adhesive on the sole doesn't exactly match the adhesive along the bite line, a bond gap could cause the shoe to fail.

After one last press with the weighted last, the still-warm sneaker enters a cooling tunnel. When the shoe emerges from the tunnel, another worker packs in a shoe form, laces up the shoe, and sends it to inspection. Finally, the completed sneaker is paired with its mate and boxed for shipment. Shoe boxes are loaded into freight containers, which are piled high on gigantic oceangoing cargo ships and sent across the Pacific Ocean. Upon docking at major US ports, sneakers travel by truck and train to stores around the country and straight onto your feet.

Hidden Costs

Globalization might mean you get a killer pair of kicks for only $100, but there's a scummy underside to global economies too. The main reason sneaker companies choose to assemble shoes in foreign countries is that labor costs are much cheaper there. The 2014 federal minimum wage in the United States was $7.25 an hour. Workers in Asian sneaker factories make around $1.25 a day.

Most of these workers are women and sometimes kids as young as thirteen, who work twelve-hour days in hot, cramped factories. Sometimes factory bosses hit workers or make them run laps if they make errors on the assembly line. Global protests against conditions in these factories have come from a wide range of interests, including labor unions, human rights groups, concerned citizens, and the US State Department. Since labor costs make up only about 12 percent of the cost of a pair of sneakers—and company profits can be as much as 22 percent of the cost of a pair of shoes—many people think these workers should be paid more.

Sneakers and the environment are not exactly best friends

either. Synthetic foam midsoles and other petroleum-based materials have a huge carbon footprint because of all the energy required to make the raw materials. Tanning leather requires treating cowhide with chemicals such as calcium hydroxide, which some shoe factories release into rivers, poisoning water plants and animals. The health-threatening chemical benzene is used to cure rubber, and some of the glues used in sneaker making are illegal in US factories because they release carcinogenic fumes that cause respiratory problems in workers.

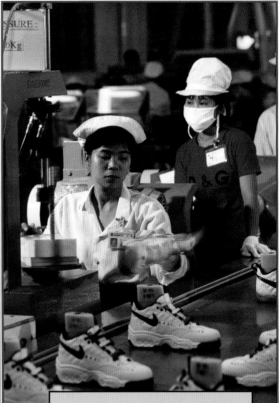

Production line workers at a NIKE factory in China assemble sneakers piece by piece. Employees at shoe factories around the globe often face long hours and poor working conditions.

Sneakers are not biodegradable either. In the spring of 1990, a cargo ship left South Korea for the United States. Storms whipped the Pacific Ocean into a frothing frenzy. Waves crashed over the huge ship and swept twenty-one containers, each 40 feet (12.2 m) long, over the edge. Five were full of Nikes—nearly forty thousand pairs in all. As the cardboard boxes disintegrated, the pairs separated and 78,932 sneakers went whirling into the currents.

American oceanographers Curtis Ebbesmeyer and W. James Ingraham took advantage of this accident to do some serious science. Each sneaker had a unique serial number, making it a perfect tracer to study ocean currents. When shoes started washing up on beaches in Hawaii, Alaska, and down the west coast of the United States all the way to California, Ebbesmeyer and Ingraham used the data they collected to analyze the movement of the North Pacific Subtropical Gyre, an ocean current that circles clockwise between Asia and North America.

Locals in Washington and Oregon took advantage of the accident. As shoes washed up on their shorelines, they set up sneaker exchanges where beachcombers could find size and style matches among the flotsam. Even after months at sea, the sneakers were in good shape, and seaside residents were soon running in style. Ten years after the spill, shoes were still washing up on the beach.

From Landfill to Turf

People around the world buy millions of sneakers. But what happens to the castoffs? Most end up in landfills. New recycling programs might change that. NIKE's Reuse-a-Shoe program turns old sneakers into a product called Grind, which can be used to make sports court surfaces and artificial turf.

Adidas is in the recycling game too. The company outfitted the seventy thousand volunteers at the 2012 London Summer Olympics in sneakers made with more than 50 percent recycled content.

Making new shoes creates a lot of waste too. After the various pieces are cut out, all the leftover scraps go straight in the trash. NIKE is pioneering a new fabric called Flyknit that is seamless, like a sock, and doesn't produce cutting waste. Adidas is working on ForMotion soles that use 50 percent less material. Both Brooks and Puma are incorporating recycled materials into new shoes.

There is no sign that sneakers are a fad on the way out. If anything, the hunger for sports shoes is growing. The person who figures out how to make greener sneakers will revolutionize the industry and further fuel the momentum of sneaker mania.

Grab Your Gutties

You've probably heard sneakers referred to as athletic shoes, cross-trainers, tennies, and kicks. As sneakers spread around the world, they picked up lots of other names too. How about some of these?

boat shoes	go-fasters	shoeclacks
bobos	grappling shoes	speed shoes
bumper boots	grips	soccer boots
daps	gutties	tackies
deck shoes	runners	tetanus shoes
felony shoes	sabogs	tread
fish heads	sandshoes	

WHERE'D YOU GET THOSE SHOES?

In a little more than one hundred years, the sneaker industry has exploded. Business is booming, thanks to the worldwide phenomenon that is sneaker culture—an amalgamation of sports, music, fashion, and business. As former Air Jordan sneaker designer D'Wayne Edwards says, "Very few products have grown every single decade and are still relevant today." Since the 1980s, the driving force behind sneakers' popularity has been urban teens, who turn athletes such as Michael Jordan into heroes and who determine what's hot and what's not in the style arena. Edwards adds, "Kids influenced everything that happened [in the history of sneakers]. Kids . . . made these companies."

Sneakerheads

Without the people who love them, sneakers are just shoes. Collectors, artists, designers, and kicks-obsessed sneaker wearers are the creative energy behind sneaker culture. These sneakerheads play important roles in all facets of the industry.

Sneaker collecting isn't just for the rich guys who drop a hundred grand on a pair of Jordans. Collectors such as fifteen-year-old Tyler Davis of Rockville Centre, New York, track limited releases, snap up the most desired pairs, and hold onto them while demand rises. With an eye for hot brands and models, Davis is a serious businessman, buying low and reselling shoes high at events such as SoleXchange sneaker conventions, which he helps organize in Long Island, New York. What's in demand changes as new designs are released.

On the Inside Track with Pensole

As a teenager in the 1980s, D'Wayne Edwards of Inglewood, California, knew he wanted to design sneakers. His high school counselor scoffed at the idea. But Edwards was determined. At nineteen he went to work for LA Gear as a file clerk. Every day he stuffed a sneaker sketch into the suggestion box with the note, "Hire me as a footwear designer" on the bottom. After six months, the company did just that! Edwards went on to design more than five hundred styles for LA Gear, Karl Kani, Skechers, and NIKE, including for the Air Jordan brand.

Since 2010 Edwards has run Pensole, a footwear design academy in Portland, Oregon. The Pensole program prepares high school and college students for jobs in the shoe industry. The academy's programs, which range from a few weeks to several months long, allow students to earn college credit toward degrees in fashion design, engineering, architecture, industrial design, and graphic design. Working in teams, students get their hands on every stage of the design process—visioning, sketching, clay modeling, material selection, hand-stitching prototypes, generating computerized design, 3-D printing, branding, and marketing strategy.

For Edwards, every sneaker is an opportunity for the designer to tell a story. "Sneakers are unlike any other product," he says, "because they influence you by touch, form, and color." As a designer, he says you want to "make people love [the shoe]." And when the shoe goes out into the world, it needs the sneakerheads, the people "who make it hot."

Shoe designer D'Wayne Edwards proudly shows off the newly released Air Jordan XX2 at the sneaker's official launch.

With more than six thousand designers in the global athletic shoe industry, new styles are coming out every week. Kid designers are doing amazing work too.

Through a collaborative program between NIKE and Doernbecher Children's Hospital in Portland, Oregon, sneakerhead cancer survivors such as Cole Johanson get to see their designs turn into real shoes. The bright-red Air Jordan 3 Retros that Johanson designed in 2010, when he was eleven, were so popular that they were rereleased in 2013.

For others, fresh-out-of-the-box kicks aren't quite what they're looking for. Armed with paint, markers, and glue-on bling, sneaker customizers turn shoes into art. Fourteen-year-old Chris Hui of Milwaukee, Wisconsin, started out buying used shoes at Goodwill, painting them in Green Bay Packers colors (green and gold), and selling them on eBay. Now he customizes high-end sneakers for celebrities such as basketball great LeBron James, talk show host Carson Daly, and rap megastar Kanye West.

Sneakerheads are serious about their kicks. The shoes on their feet are part of their identity and are a form of self-expression. When they ask, "Where'd you get those shoes?" they're really asking "Who are you?" and "What are you passionate about?" Sneakerhead sports fans might wear sneakers designed by their favorite player. The fashion conscious might stick with bling-covered wedge heels. You can even get cutesy—designer Jeremy Scott teamed up with Adidas to make sneakers with stuffed animal heads attached.

Whatever the obsession, sneakerheads bring it onto the basketball court and through the halls at school. Sneakerheads are athletes and artists, musicians and radicals, designers and entrepreneurs—and their passion is one of the driving forces behind the future of sneakers.

Source Notes

5 Matthew Piper, "Ex-Jazz Ball Boy Selling Jordan's Shoes from Legendary 'Flu Game,'" *Salt Lake Tribune*, November 13, 2013.

14 Frederick W. Robinson, *Female Life in Prison* (Toronto: Rose Publishing Company, 1888), 150.

29 J. B. Strasser and Laurie Becklund, *Swoosh: The Unauthorized Story of Nike and the Men Who Played There* (San Diego: Harcourt Brace Jovanovich, 1991), 17.

30 Gerald Jonas, Grover Amen, and Brendan Gill, "The Talk of the Town, 'Revolution,'" *New Yorker*, May 12, 1962, 34–35.

30 Ibid.

39 "Air Jordan 1 Commercial—Man Was Not Meant to FLY," YouTube video, 0:29, posted by "KicksOnFirecom", February 28, 2010, http://www.youtube.com /watch?v=pvtTwZpf-P0.

44 Josh Feit, "The Nike Psyche," *Willamette Week*, May 28, 1997.

45 D'Wayne Edwards, interview with author, December 18, 2013.

50 Eric Graham, interview with author, June 12, 2013.

50 Ibid.

55 Edwards interview.

55 Ibid.

56 Ibid.

56 Ibid.

56 Ibid.

56 Ibid.

Selected Bibliography

Bramble, Dennis, and Daniel Lieberman. "Endurance Running and the Evolution of Homo." *Nature*, November 18, 2004, 345–352.

Cheskin, Melvyn. *The Complete Handbook of Athletic Footwear.* New York: Fairchild Publications, 1987.

Connolly, Thomas, Petr Hlavacek, Kenny Moore, Jon Erlandson, and Brian Lanker. *10,000 Years of Shoes.* Edited by Sarah McClure. Eugene: University of Oregon Press, 2011.

Diaz, Angel. "The 20 Most Iconic Sneakers in Olympic History." *Sneaker Report,* August 10, 2012. http://sneakerreport.com/news/the-20-most-iconic-sneakers-in -olympic-history.

Ebbesmeyer, Curt, and Eric Scigliano. *Flotsametrics and the Floating World: How One Man's Obsession with Runaway Sneakers and Rubber Ducks Revolutionized Ocean Science.* New York: Smithsonian Books and HarperCollins, 2009.

Hamilton, Anita. "Freaking for Sneakers." *Time Magazine*, March 13, 2006, 42.

Hines, Alice. "Meet the New Teen Sneakerheads: Flipping Shoes for Cash, Fast." *NYMAG.com*, March 4, 2013. http://nymag.com/thecut/2013/03/new-teen -sneakerheads-making-thousands-fast.html.

Jorgensen, Janice, ed. *Encyclopedia of Consumer Brands.* Detroit: St. James Press, 1994.

McDougall, Christopher. *Born to Run: A Hidden Tribe, Superathletes, and the Greatest Race the World Has Never Seen.* New York: Alfred A. Knopf, 2009.

Palladino, Grace. *Teenagers: An American History.* New York: HarperCollins, 1996.

Piper, Matthew. "Ex-Jazz Ball Boy Selling Jordan's Shoes from Legendary 'Flu Game.'" *Salt Lake Tribune*, November 13, 2013.

Schaap, Jeremy. *Triumph: The Jesse Owens Story.* Boston: Houghton Mifflin, 2007.

Smit, Barbara. *Sneaker Wars: The Enemy Brothers Who Founded Adidas and Puma and the Family Feud That Forever Changed the Business of Sports.* New York: HarperCollins, 2008.

Staple, Jeff. "The Fifty Most Influential People in Sneaker History." *Complex,* August 14, 2012. http://www.complex.com/sneakers/2012/08/the-50-most -influential-people-in-sneaker-history.

Strasser, J. B., and Laurie Becklund. *Swoosh: The Unauthorized Story of Nike and the Men Who Played There.* San Diego: Harcourt Brace Jovanovich, 1991.

Vanderbilt, Tom. *The Sneaker Book: Anatomy of an Industry and an Icon.* New York: The New Press, 1998.

For More Information

Burns, Loree Griffin. *Tracking Trash: Flotsam, Jetsam, and the Science of Ocean Motion.* New York: HMH Books for Young Readers, 2007. This *School Library Journal* star-reviewed book in HMH's Scientists in the Field series takes a look at oceanographer Curtis Ebbesmeyer, who noticed flotsam (trash) washing up on the shore near his home in Seattle, Washington. By studying the path of floating sneakers and other items that had fallen off oceangoing container ships, Ebbesmeyer and his colleague W. James Ingraham tracked the currents of the ocean. Their experiments and data have exposed how debris pollutes the oceans and harms marine life.

Complex
http://www.complex.com
Explore streetwear and sneaker culture on this design site. Great articles include "The 50 Most Influential People in Sneaker History" and "20 Sneaker Customizers You Need to Know."

Female Sneaker Fiend
http://www.femalesneakerfiend.com
At this site, you can connect with other sneaker-obsessed women, female footwear designers, and some of the hippest voices in sneaker culture of the twenty-first century.

Girls Got Kicks
http://www.girlsgotkicks.com
Dive into the world of female sneakerheads with this photo documentary and blog devoted to girls and women who express themselves with their kicks.

Kicks on Fire
http://www.kicksonfire.com
Visitors can track new kicks from all the major brands at sneakerhead central.

Obsessive Sneaker Disorder
http://www.osdlive.com
Get sneaker news from weekly podcasts with important players in the sneaker industry and the entertainment world. Obsessive Sneaker Disorder also offers an eight-week workshop about sneakers for young people called SOLEcial Studies: Sneakers, Their Impact on Lifestyles, Culture, and People in the 21st Century.

Osborne, Ben, ed. *SLAM Kicks: Basketball Sneakers That Changed the Game*. New York: Universe, 2014. Edited by Ben Osborne, the editor in chief of the American basketball publication *SLAM Magazine*, this book offers an informative overview and photos of legendary basketball shoes and their designs. Readers learn about technical advancements, the athletes who made the shoes famous, and cultural impact of the kicks.

Sneaker Report
http://www.sneakerreport.com
Track sneaker releases and read interesting articles such as "The 20 Most Iconic Sneakers in Olympic History."

Unorthodox Styles. *Sneakers: The Complete Collectors' Guide*. London: Thames & Hudson, 2005. This book is a great introduction for sneakerheads to a wide range of different models and brands of athletic shoes, complete with colorful photos.

Index

Photo Acknowledgments

The images in this book are used with the permission of: © FreeBirdPhotos /Shutterstock.com, (shoestring); © Sean O' Dwyer/Shutterstock.com, (shoeprint) (closeup shoeprint); © evastudio/Shutterstock.com, p. 4; © Steve Schaefer/AFP /Getty Images, p. 5; © Richard Newstead/Moment/Getty Images, p. 8; © Sandro Vannini/CORBIS, p. 10; Markus Brinkmann/Wikimedia Commons (CC BY-SA 2.0), p. 12; Colchester Rubber Company/Wikimedia Commons (public domain), p. 13; © Todd Strand/Independent Picture Service, p. 14; North Carolina State University, (public domain), p. 16; © Ragnarock/Shutterstock.com, p. 18; © Joe Klamar/AFP /Getty Images, p. 19; © Per-Anders Pettersson/CORBIS, p. 20; © Popperfoto /Getty Images, p. 24; © UPI/dpa/CORBIS, p. 25; © Lenscap/Alamy, p. 28; ©Pictorial Press Ltd/Alamy, p. 31; © AFP/Getty Images, p. 32; © Mickey Maker /The Denver Post via Getty Images, p. 36; © Andrew Buckin/Shutterstock.com, p. 39; © Michael Ochs Archives/Getty Images, p. 40; © Michel Dufour/WireImage /Getty Images, p. 44; © Julian Finney/Getty Images, p. 45; © snimau/iStock /Thinkstock, p. 46; © Splash/PMKCustoms.com/Splash News/CORBIS, p. 48; © Jamieson Parker of "Ikonic Artistry," p. 49; © Peter Charlesworth/LightRocket via Getty Images, p. 52; © Phillip Roberts/Alamy, p. 54; Steve Marcus/Reuters /Newscom, p. 56.

Front cover: © Ragnarock/Shutterstock.com.

About the Author

Amber J. Keyser is a former ballerina and evolutionary biologist who writes both fiction and nonfiction for tweens and teens. She is drawn to heartfelt stories about quirky scientists, everyday heroes, and the adventurer in each of us. Keyser is the author of the picture book *An Algonquin Heart Song: Paddle My Own Canoe*, two graphic novels about science in the Max Axiom series, and the nonfiction title *Anatomy of a Pandemic*. She wields pen and pitchfork from Portland, Oregon, where she lives on a mini-farm with her husband, two children, and a flock of charismatic chickens. Learn more about her at www.amberjkeyser.com.